Guitar • Vocal

T0088316

CHRISTMAS CAROLS

Lyrics, Chord Symbols and
Guitar Chord Diagrams for 40 Favorites

ISBN 978-1-5400-9741-5

Visit Hal Leonard Online at
www.halleonard.com

Contact us:
Hal Leonard
7777 West Bluemound Road
Milwaukee, WI 53213
Email: info@halleonard.com

In Europe, contact:
Hal Leonard Europe Limited
42 Wigmore Street
Marylebone, London, W1U 2RN
Email: info@halleonardeurope.com

In Australia, contact:
Hal Leonard Australia Pty. Ltd.
4 Lentara Court
Cheltenham, Victoria, 3192 Australia
Email: info@halleonard.com.au

Contents

Angels from the Realms of Glory

Words by James Montgomery
Music by Henry T. Smart

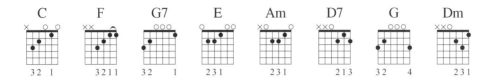

Verse 1

C | |
Angels from the realms of glory,

F **C** |**G7** **C** |
Wing your flight o'er all the earth;

| **E** |
Ye who sang cre - ation's sto - ry,

Am |**D7** **G** ‖
Now proclaim Mes - siah's birth.

Chorus 1

G7 |
Come and worship!

C **F** |
Come and worship!

Dm |**G7** **C** ‖
Worship Christ the newborn King!

Verse 2

```
C                    |              |
Shepherds in the fields abiding,
F        C      |G7      C      |
Watching o'er your flocks by night,
                 |      E        |
God with man is now re - siding;
Am               |D7   G      ‖
Yonder shines the infant Light.
```

Chorus 2   *Repeat Chorus 1*

Verse 3

```
C                    |              |
Sages, leave your contemplations,
F        C      |G7      C      |
Brighter visions beam a - far,
                 |      E         |
Seek the great De - sire of Nations,
Am               |D7   G      ‖
Ye have seen His natal star.
```

Chorus 3   *Repeat Chorus 1*

Verse 4

```
C                    |              |
Saints before the altar bending,
F        C      |G7      C      |
Watching long in hope and fear,
                 |      E        |
Suddenly the Lord, de - scending,
Am               |D7     G      ‖
In His temple shall ap - pear.
```

Chorus 4   *Repeat Chorus 1*

Angels We Have Heard on High

Traditional French Carol
Translated by James Chadwick

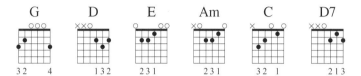

Verse 1

G |D   G |
Angels we have heard on high

      |D   G |
Sweetly singing o'er the plains,

       |D   G |
And the mountains in re - ply

      |D   G   ‖
Echoing their joyous strains.

Chorus 1

G E |Am D |G C |D   D7 |
Glo -   ri - a

G D G   C |G D |
In ex - cel - sis De - o,

G E |Am D |G C |D   D7 |
Glo -   ri - a

G D G   C |G D7 |G   ‖
In ex - cel - sis De - o.

Verse 2

G |D G |
Shepherds, why this jubi - lee?

        |D   G |
Why your joyous strains pro - long?

        |D   G |
What the gladsome tidings be

         |D   G ||
Which inspire your heav'nly song?

Chorus 2   *Repeat Chorus 1*

G |D G |
Verse 3   Come to Bethle - hem and see

        |D   G |
Him whose birth the angels sing.

       |D   G |
Come adore on bended knee

        |D   G ||
Christ the Lord, the newborn King.

Chorus 3   *Repeat Chorus 1*

G |D G |
Verse 4   See within a manger laid

       |D   G |
Jesus, Lord of heav'n and earth!

       |D   G |
Mary, Joseph, lend your aid,

        |D   G ||
With us sing our Savior's birth.

Chorus 4   *Repeat Chorus 1*

As with Gladness Men of Old

Words by William Chatterton Dix
Music by Conrad Kocher

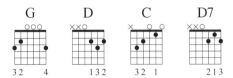

Verse 1

G   D   G |C D7 G |
As with glad - ness men of old

C   G   C |D   G |
Did the guid - ing star be - hold;

D G |C   D7 G |
As with joy they hailed its light,

C   G   C |D   G |
Leading on - ward, beaming bright;

|D   G |
So, most gracious Lord, may we

C   G   C |G D G ||
Ever - more be led to Thee.

Verse 2

G   D   G |C D7 G |
As with joy - ful steps they sped

C   G   C |D   G |
To that low - ly manger bed,

D   G |C   D7 G |
There to bend the knee be - fore

C   G   C |D   G |
Him whom heav'n and earth a - dore;

|D   G |
So may we with willing feet

C   G   C |G   D   G ||
Ever seek thy mer - cy seat.

Verse 3

G   D G |C D7 G |
As they of - fered gifts most rare

C   G   C |D   G |
At that man - ger rude and bare;

        D G |C D7 G |
So may we with ho - ly   joy,

C   G C |D   G |
Pure and free from sin's al - loy,

                 |D   G |
All our costliest treasures bring,

C   G   C |G   D G ||
Christ, to Thee, our heav'n - ly   King.

Verse 4

G D G |C D7 G |
Holy Je - sus, ev - 'ry   day

C   G C |D   G |
Keep us in the narrow way;

      D   G |C   D7 G |
And when earth - ly things are past,

C   G   C |D   G |
Bring our ran - somed souls at last

              |D   G |
Where they need no star to guide,

C   G   C |G D G ||
Where no clouds Thy glo - ry hide.

Auld Lang Syne

Words by Robert Burns
Traditional Scottish Melody

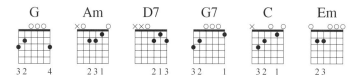

Verse

    ‖**G** |**Am** **D7**
Should auld acquaintance be for - got

   |**G** **G7** |**C**
And never brought to mind?

   |**G**   **Em** |**Am** **D7**
Should auld ac - quaintance be for - got

   |**Em** **Am** **D7** |**G**
And days of Auld Lang Syne?

   | **Em** |**Am**   **D7**
For Auld Lang Syne, my dear,

   |**G** **G7** |**C**
For Auld Lang Syne,

   |**G** **Em** |**Am**   **D7**
We'll tak' a cup o' kindness yet,

   |**Em Am D7** |**G**   ‖
For Auld Lang ___ Syne.

Away in a Manger

Traditional
Words by John T. McFarland (v.3)
Music by William J. Kirkpatrick

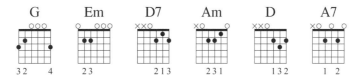

Verse 1

‖G |Em |G |D7
A - way in a manger, no crib for a bed,

|Am D |G |A7 |D
The little Lord Jesus laid down His sweet head.

|G |Em |G |D7
The stars in the bright sky looked down where He lay,

|Am D |G |Am   D7 |G
The little Lord Jesus a - sleep on the hay.

Verse 2

‖G |Em |G |D7
The cattle are lowing, the baby a - wakes,

|Am D |G |A7 |D
But little Lord Jesus, no crying He makes.

|G |Em |G |D7
I love Thee, Lord Jesus, look down from the sky,

|Am D |G |Am   D7 |G
And stay by my side until morning is neigh.

Verse 3

‖G |Em |G |D7
Be near me, Lord Jesus; I ask Thee to stay

|Am D |G |A7 |D
Close by me for - ever and love me, I pray.

|G |Em |G |D7
Bless all the dear children in Thy tender care,

|Am D |G |Am   D7 |G   ‖
And fit us for heaven to live with Thee there.

Away in a Manger

Words by John T. McFarland (v.3)
Music by James R. Murray

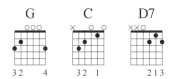

Verse 1

‖G | |C |G
A - way in a manger, no crib for a bed,
 |D7 | |G |
The little Lord Jesus laid down His sweet head.
 | | |C |G
The stars in the sky looked down where He lay,
 |D7 |G |C   D7 |G
The little Lord Jesus, a - sleep on the hay.

Verse 2

‖G | |C |G
The cattle are lowing, the Baby a - wakes,
 |D7 | |G |
But little Lord Jesus no crying He makes.
 | | |C |G
I love Thee, Lord Jesus, look down from the sky,
 |D7 |G |C   D7 |G
And stay by my cradle till morning is nigh.

Verse 3

‖G | |C |G
Be near me, Lord Jesus, I ask Thee to stay
 |D7 | |G |
Close by me for - ever and love me, I pray.
 | | |C |G
Bless all the dear children in Thy tender care,
 |D7 |G |C   D7 |G ‖
And fit us for heaven to live with Thee there.

Bring a Torch, Jeannette, Isabella

17th Century French Provencal Carol

G	Em	Am	D7	C

Verse 1

G |Em |Am |D7 |
Bring a torch, Jean - nette Isa - bella,

G |Em |D7 |G |
Bring a torch, come swiftly and run.

| | |D7 |
Christ is born, tell the folk of the village,

C |G |C |D7 |Em |D7 |
Jesus is sleeping in His cradle, ah, ah,

G |D7 |G |Em |D7 |
Beautiful is the Mother, ah, ah,

G |D7 |G | ‖
Beautiful is Her Son.

Verse 2

G |Em |Am |D7 |
Hasten now, good folk of the village,

G |Em |D7 |G |
Hasten now, the Christ Child to see.

| | |D7 |
You will find him a - sleep in a manger,

C |G |C |D7 |Em |D |
Quietly come and whisper softly, hush, hush,

G |D7 |G |Em |D7 |
Peacefully now He slumbers, hush, hush,

G |D7 |G | ‖
Peacefully now He sleeps.

Christ Was Born on Christmas Day

Traditional

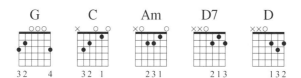

Verse 1

G | C G |
Christ was born on Christ - mas Day,

| C G |
Wreath the holly, twine the bay;

Am D7 |G D
Christus natus hodi - e;

|G C |G D7 |G ‖
The Babe, the Son, the Holy One of Mary.

Verse 2

G | C G |
He was born to set us free,

| C G |
He was born our Lord to be,

Am D7 |G D
Ex Ma - ria virgi - ne;

|G C | D7 |G ‖
The God, the Lord, by all a - dored for - ever.

Verse 3

G | C G |
Let the bright red ber - ries glow,

| C G |
Ev'rywhere in good - ly show;

Am D7 |G D
Christus natus hodi - e;

|G C |G D7 |G ‖
The Babe, the Son, the Holy One of Mary.

Verse 4

G | C G |
Christain men re - joice and sing,

| C G |
'Tis the birthday of a King.

Am D7 |G D
Ex Ma - ria virgi - ne;

|G C | D7 |G ‖
The God, the Lord, by all a - dored for - ever.

Come, Thou Long-Expected Jesus

Words by Charles Wesley
Music by Rowland Hugh Prichard

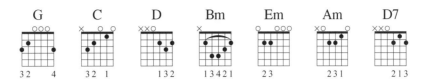

Verse 1

G | |C |D |
Come Thou long-ex - pected Jesus,

G | |D |G |
Born to set Thy people free.

| |C |D |
From our fears and sins re - lease us,

G | |D |G |
Let us find our rest in Thee.

Bm |Em |Am |D7 |
Israel's strength and conso - lation,

G |Em |Am |D |
Hope of all the earth Thou art.

G |D7 |G |D7 |
Dear de - sire of ev'ry nation,

G |C |D7 |G ‖
Joy of ev'ry longing heart.

Verse 2

G | |C |D |
Born Thy people to de - liver,

G | |D |G |
Born a child and yet a king.

| |C |D |
Born to reign in us for - ever,

G | |D |G |
Now Thy gracious kingdom bring.

Bm |Em |Am |D7 |
By Thine own e - ternal Spirit,

G |Em |Am |D |
Rule in all our hearts a - lone.

G |D7 |G |D7 |
By Thine all suf - ficient merit,

G |C |D7 |G ‖
Raise us to Thy glorious throne.

Coventry Carol

Words by Robert Croo
Traditional English Melody

Dm   C   A   Gm   D

Verse 1

Dm | |**C** |**A** |
Lullay, thou little tiny Child,

Dm |**Gm** |**Dm** |
By by, lul - ly lul - lay.

          |**C** | |**Gm** |**A** |
Lul - lay, thou little tiny   Child,

Dm |**Gm** |**D** | ||
By by, lul - ly lul - lay.

Verse 2

Dm | |**C** |**A** |
O sisters too, how may we do,

Dm |**Gm** |**Dm** |
For to pre - serve this day.

          |**C** | |**Gm** |**A** |
This poor young - ling for whom we sing,

Dm |**Gm** |**D** | ||
By by, lul - ly lul - lay.

Verse 3

Dm | |**C** |**A** |
Herod the king, in his rag - ing,

Dm |**Gm** |**Dm** |
Charged he hath this day.

          |**C** | |**Gm** |**A** |
His men of might, in his own sight,

Dm |**Gm** |**D** | ||
All young chil - dren to slay.

Verse 4

Dm | |**C** |**A** |
That woe is me, poor Child for Thee!

Dm |**Gm** |**Dm** |
And ever morn and day,

          |**C** | |**Gm** |**A** |
For thy part - ing nor say nor sing,

Dm |**Gm** |**D** | ||
By by, lul - ly lul - lay.

Jingle Bells

Words and Music by
J. Pierpont

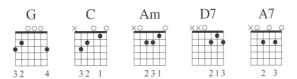

Verse 1

G | | |**C** |
Dashing through the snow, in a one horse open sleigh,

Am |**D7** | |**G** |
O'er the fields we go,   laughing all the way.

| | |**C**
Bells on bobtail ring, making spirits bright,

|**Am** |**G** |**D7** |**G** ‖
What fun it is to ride and sing a sleighing song to - night.

Chorus 1

G | | | |
Jingle bells, jingle bells, jingle all the way!

C |**G** |**A7** |**D7** |
Oh, what fun it is to ride in a one horse open sleigh! Oh!

G | | | |
Jingle bells, jingle bells, jingle all the way!

C |**G** |**D7** |**G**
Oh, what fun it is to ride in a one horse open sleigh!

Verse 2

‖**G** | | |**C**
A day or two a - go I thought I'd take a ride,

|**Am** |**D7** | |**G**
And soon Miss Fannie Bright was sitting by my side.

| | | |**C**
The horse was lean and lank, mis - fortune seemed his lot,

|**Am** |**G** |**D7** |**G** ‖
He got into a drifted bank and we, we got up - shot.

Chorus 2

Repeat Chorus 1

Deck the Hall

Traditional Welsh Carol

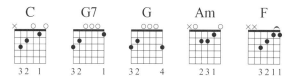

Verse 1

C | |
Deck the hall with boughs of holly,
G7 C |G C |
Fa la la la la, la la la la.

| |
'Tis the season to be jolly,
G7 C |G C |
Fa la la la la, la la la la.

G7 |C G |
Don we now our gay appar - el,
C Am |G G7|
Fa la la la la la la la la.
C | |
Troll the ancient Yuletide carol,
F C |G C ||
Fa la la la la, la la la la.

Verse 2

```
C                    |              |
See the blazing Yule before us,
G7      C    |G   C   |
Fa la la la la, la la la la.

                     |              |
Strike the harp and join the chorus,
G7      C    |G   C   |
Fa la la la la, la la la la.
G7          |C        G    |
Follow me in merry meas - ure,
C     Am  |G    G7|
Fa la la la la la la la la,
C                    |              |
While I tell of Yuletide treasure,
F        C   |G   C   ‖
Fa la la la la, la la la la.
```

Verse 3

```
C                    |              |
Fast away the old year passes,
G7      C    |G   C   |
Fa la la la la, la la la la.

                     |              |
Hail the new, ye lads and lasses,
G7      C    |G   C   |
Fa la la la la, la la la la.
G7           |C        G   |
Sing we joyous all togeth - er,
C     Am  |G    G7|
Fa la la la la la la la la,
C                    |              |
Heedless of the wind and weather,
F        C   |G   C   ‖
Fa la la la la, la la la la.
```

Ding Dong! Merrily on High!

French Carol

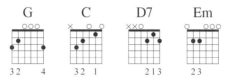

Verse 1

G |
Ding dong! Merrily on high
|**C**   **D7** |**G** |
In heav'n the bells are ringing.

|
Ding dong! Verily the sky
|**C**   **D7** |**G** ||
Is riv'n with angel singing.

Chorus 1

G |**D7** |**Em** |**D7** |**Em** |**D7**
Glo   -   ria,
|**C**   **D7** |**G** |
Ho - sanna in ex - celsis!
     |**D7** |**Em** |**D7** |**Em** |**D7**
Glo   -   ria,
|**C**   **D7** |**G** ||
Ho - sanna in ex - celsis!

Verse 2

G |
E'en so here below, be - low,
  |C   D7 |G |
Let steeple bells be swungen,
          |
And i-o, i-o, i - o,
  |C   D7 |G   ‖
By priest and people sungen.

Chorus 2   *Repeat Chorus 1*

Verse 3

G |
Pray you, dutifully prime
     |C   D7 |G |
Your matin chime, ye ringers,
          |
May you beautifully rime
     |C   D7 |G   ‖
Your eve-time song, ye singers.

Chorus 3   *Repeat Chorus 1*

The First Noel

17th Century English Carol
Music from W. Sandys' Christmas Carols

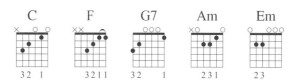

Verse 1

```
 ‖C        |      |F      |C
The first No - el the angels did say
       |F         |C          |G7        |C
Was to certain poor shepherds in fields as they lay.
   |         |       |F         |C
In fields where they lay keeping their sheep
   |F         |C       |G7  |C
On a cold winter's night that was so deep.
```

Chorus 1

```
   ‖C   |Em   |F      |C        |
No - el, No - el, No - e l, No - e l,
F           |C     |G7    |C
Born is the King of Isra  -  el.
```

Verse 2

```
   ‖C        |      |F    |C
They looked up and saw a star
       |F   |C      |G7        |C
Shining in the East be - yond them far,
   |      |      |F         |C
And to the earth it gave great light,
   |F       |C       |G7      |C
And so it con - tinued both day and night.
```

Chorus 2 *Repeat Chorus 1*

Verse 3

```
        ‖ C    |       |F        |C
And by the light of that same star
        |F       |C          |G7   |C
Three wise men came from country far.
        |        |        |F      |C
To seek for a king was their in - tent,
        |F       |C         |G7   |C
And to follow the star wher - ever it went.
```

Chorus 3 *Repeat Chorus 1*

Verse 4

```
        ‖ C      |       |F        |C
This star drew nigh to the north - west,
        |F     |C    |G7      |C
O'er Bethle-hem it took its rest.
        |        |        |F        |C
And there it did both stop and stay
        |F       |C          |G7   |C
Right over the place where Jesus  lay.
```

Chorus 4 *Repeat Chorus 1*

Go, Tell It on the Mountain

African-American Spiritual
Verses by John W. Work, Jr.

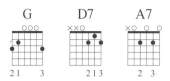

Chorus 1

G
Go tell it on the mountain,
D7 |**G**
Over the hills and ev'rywhere;

Go tell it on the mountain
   | **D7** |**G**
That Jesus Christ is born.

Verse 1

  ‖**G**
While shepherds kept their watching
 |**D7** |**G**
O'er silent flocks by night,

Be - hold, throughout the heavens,
  |**A7** |**D7**   ‖
There shone a holy light.

Chorus 2   *Repeat Chorus 1*

Verse 2

‖ **G** |
The shepherds feared and trembled
| **D7** | **G**
When, lo! above the earth

| |
Rang out the angel chorus
| **A7** | **D7**   ‖
That hailed our Savior's birth.

Chorus 3   *Repeat Chorus 1*

Verse 3

‖ **G** |
Down in a lowly manger
| **D7** | **G**
The humble Christ was born,

| |
And God sent us sal - vation
| **A7** | **D7**   ‖
That blessed Christmas morn.

Chorus 4   *Repeat Chorus 1*

God Rest Ye Merry, Gentlemen

Traditional English Carol

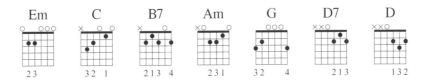

Verse 1

‖**Em** |
God rest ye merry, gentlemen,

|**C** |**B7**
Let nothing you dis - may,

|**Em** |
Re - member Christ our Saviour

|**C** |**B7**
Was born on Christmas Day,

|**Am** |**G**
To save us all from Satan's pow'r

|**Em** |**D7**
When we were gone a - stray.

Chorus 1

‖**G** |**B7** |**Em** |**D**
O tidings of comfort and joy, comfort and joy,

|**G** |**B7** |**Em**
O tidings of comfort and joy.

Verse 2

‖**Em** |
In Bethlehem, in Jewry,

|**C** |**B7**
This blessed Babe was born,

|**Em** |
And laid within a manger

|**C** |**B7**
Up - on this blessed morn,

|**Am** |**G**
That which His Mother Mary

|**Em** |**D7**
Did nothing take in scorn.

Chorus 2   *Repeat Chorus 1*

Verse 3

‖**Em** |
From God our heav'nly Father

|**C** |**B7**
A blessed angel came,

|**Em** |
And unto certain shepherds

|**C** |**B7**
Brought tidings of the same,

|**Am** |**G**
How that in Bethle - hem was born

|**Em** |**D7**
The Son of God by name.

Chorus 3   *Repeat Chorus 1*

Good Christian Men, Rejoice

14th Century Latin Text
Translated by John Mason Neale
14th Century German Melody

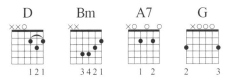

Verse 1

‖**D** |
Good Christian men, re - joice,

| | |
With heart and soul and voice;

|**Bm** |
Give ye heed to what we say:

D |**A7** |**D** |
News! News! Jesus Christ is born today!

|**Bm** |
Ox and ass be - fore Him bow,

|**A7** |**D** |
And He is in the manger now;

G **A7** |**Bm** **G** |
Christ is born to - day!_____

D **A7** |**D**
Christ is born to - day!

Verse 2

```
    ‖ D                 |
Good Christian men, re - joice,
      |                  |                 |
With heart and soul and voice;
                    | Bm               |
Now ye hear of endless bliss;
D       | A7              | D             |
Joy! Joy! Jesus Christ was born for this!
                    | Bm
He has opened heaven's door,
    | A7              | D             |
And man is blessed evermore.
G            A7      | Bm    G  |
Christ was born for this!____
D            A7      | D
Christ was born for this!
```

Verse 3

```
    ‖ D                 |
Good Christian men, re - joice,
      |                  |                 |
With heart and soul and voice;
                    | Bm               |
Now ye need not fear the grave;
D              | A7              | D             |
Peace! Peace! Jesus Christ was born to save!
                    | Bm
Calls you one and calls you all,
    | A7              | D             |
To gain His ever - lasting hall.
G            A7      | Bm    G  |
Christ was born to save!____
D            A7      | D           ‖
Christ was born to save!
```

Good King Wenceslas

Words by John M. Neale
Music from Piae Cantiones

Verse 1

G | |
Good King Wences - las looked out
C   **D7** |**G** |
On the feast of Stephen,

        | |
When the snow lay 'round about,
C   **D7** |**G** |
Deep and crisp and even.

       | **Em** |
Brightly shone the moon that night,
C   **D7** |**G** |
Though the frost was cruel,

       |**Em**   **D7** |
When a poor man came in sight,
G |**C** |**G**   ‖
Gath'ring winter fu - el.

Verse 2

```
      G                |              |
"Hither, page, and stand by me,
C        D7        |G           |
If thou know'st it, telling,

                      |              |
Yonder peasant, who is he?
C           D7        |G           |
Where and what his dwelling?"

                      |         Em     |
"Sire, he lives a good league hence,
C        D7        |G           |
Under - neath the mountain,

                      |Em    D7    |
Right against the forest fence,
G                |C     |G       ‖
By Saint Agnes' foun  -  tain."
```

Verse 3

```
      G                |              |
"Bring me flesh and bring me wine,
C        D7        |G           |
Bring me pine logs hither.

                      |              |
Thou and I will see him dine
C        D7        |G           |
When we bear them thither."

                      |          Em     |
Page and monarch, forth they went,
C        D7        |G           |
Forth they went to - gether,

                      |Em      D7      |
Through the rude wind's wild la - ment
G                |C     |G       ‖
And the bitter weath - er.
```

Hark! The Herald Angels Sing

Words by Charles Wesley
Altered by George Whitefield
Music by Felix Mendelssohn-Bartholdy
Arranged by William H. Cummings

Verse 1

C | **G7** |
Hark! The herald angels sing,

 C   F |**C   G7   C** |
"Glory to the new - born King!

 |**Am   D7** |
Peace on earth and mercy mild,

G | **D7   G** |
God and sinners rec - on - ciled."

C |**G7** |
Joyful all ye nations, rise,

C |**G7** |
Join the triumph of the skies.

F   **A7** |**Dm** |
With th'angel - ic   host proclaim,

G7   C | **G7   C** |
Christ is born in Beth - le - hem.

F   **A7** |**Dm** |
Hark! The her - ald   angels sing,

 G7   C | **G7   C** ‖
"Glory to the new - born King!"

Verse 2

C | G7 |
Christ, by highest heav'n a - dored,

C   F | C   G7   C |
Christ, the ever - last - ing   Lord.

|Am   D7 |
Late in time be - hold Him come,

G | D7   G |
Offspring of the vir - gin's womb.

C |G7 |
Veil'd in flesh the Godhead see,

C |G7 |
Hail th'Incarnate Deity.

F   A7 |Dm |
Pleased as Man with man to dwell,

G7   C | G7   C |
Jesus our Em - man - u - el!

F   A7 |Dm |
Hark! The her - ald   angels sing,

G7   C | G7   C ‖
"Glory to the new - born King!"

Here We Come A-Wassailing

Traditional

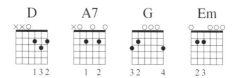

Verse 1

D
Here we come a-wassailing

           A7 |**D**
A - mong the leaves so green;

G |**D**
Here we come a-wandering,

  |**Em** |**A7**
So fair to be seen.

Refrain 1

        ‖**D G** |**D**
Love and joy come to you,

A7 |**D**   **G** |**D**
And to you, your wassail too:

A7 |**D G** |**A7**
And God bless you and send you

 |**D** |**G**
A happy New Year,

     |**D** **Em** |**A7** |**D** | ‖
And God send you a happy New Year.

Verse 2

```
D                |
We are not daily beggars
         |         A7    |D         |
That beg from door to door,
G                    |D
But we are neighbor children
      |Em           |A7
Whom you have seen be - fore.
```

Refrain 2

Repeat Refrain 1

Verse 3

```
D                |
We have got a little purse
      |         A7    |D
Of stretching leather skin;
   |G          |D
We want a little money
   |Em           |A7
To line it well with - in.
```

Refrain 3

Repeat Refrain 1

Verse 4

```
  ‖D                |
God bless the master of this house;
      |         A7    |D         |
Like - wise the mistress, too;
G          |D
And the little children
      |Em           |A7
That 'round the table go.
```

Refrain 4

Repeat Refrain 1

I Heard the Bells on Christmas Day

Words by Henry Wadsworth Longfellow
Music by John Baptiste Calkin

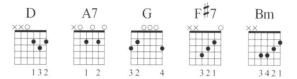

Verse 1

‖D |A7
I heard the bells on Christmas Day,

  |D |A7
Their old familiar carols play,

  |G |F#7   Bm
And wild and sweet the words re - peat

  |D |A7   D
Of peace on earth, good will to men.

Verse 2

‖D |A7
I thought how, as the day had come,

  |D |A7
The belfries of all Christendom

  |G |F#7   Bm
Had rolled along the un - broken song

  |D |A7   D
Of peace on earth, good will to men.

Verse 3

  ‖**D** |**A7**
And in despair I bow'd my head.

   |**D** |**A7**
"There is no peace on earth," I said,

   |**G** |**F♯7** **Bm**
"For hate is strong and mocks the song

   |**D** |**A7** **D**
Of peace on earth, good will to men."

Verse 4

   ‖**D** |**A7**
Then pealed the bells more loud and deep:

   |**D** |**A7**
"God is not dead, nor doth He sleep.

   |**G** |**F♯7** **Bm**
The wrong shall fail, the right pre - vail,

   |**D** |**A7** **D**
With peace on earth, good will to men."

Verse 5

   ‖**D** |**A7**
Till ringing, singing, on its way,

   |**D** |**A7**
The world revolved from night to day.

  |**G** |**F♯7** **Bm**
A voice, a chime, a chant sub - lime

   |**D** |**A7** **D** ‖
Of peace on earth, good will to men!

I Saw Three Ships

Traditional English Carol

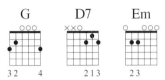

Verse 1

‖**G** |
I saw three ships come sailing in
| |**D7**
On Christmas Day, on Christmas Day.
|**G** |
I saw three ships come sailing in
| **Em** |**D7** **G**
On Christmas Day in the morn - ing.

Verse 2

‖**G** |
And what was in those ships all three
| |**D7**
On Christmas Day, on Christmas Day?
|**G** |
And what was in those ships all three
| **Em** |**D7** **G**
On Christmas Day in the morn - ing?

Verse 3

   ‖**G** |
Our Saviour Christ and His lady,

  | |**D7**
On Christmas Day, on Christmas Day.

   |**G** |
Our Saviour Christ and His lady,

  | **Em** |**D7**   **G**
On Christmas Day in the morn - ing.

Verse 4

   ‖**G** |
Pray, whither sailed those ships all three

  | |**D7**
On Christmas Day, on Christmas Day?

    |**G** |
Pray, whither sailed those ships all three

  | **Em** |**D7**   **G**
On Christmas Day in the morn - ing?

Verse 5

  ‖**G** |
O, they sailed into Bethlehem

  | |**D7**
On Christmas Day, on Christmas Day.

  |**G** |
O, they sailed into Bethlehem

  | **Em** |**D7**   **G**
On Christmas Day in the morn - ing.

Verse 6

   ‖**G** |
And all the bells on earth shall ring

  | |**D7**
On Christmas Day, on Christmas Day.

  |**G** |
And all the bells on earth shall ring

  | **Em** |**D7**   **G**   ‖
On Christmas Day in the morn - ing.

It Came Upon the Midnight Clear

Words by Edmund Hamilton Sears
Music by Richard Storrs Willis

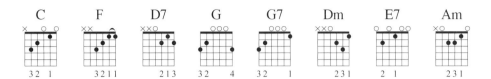

Verse 1

```
‖C      |F    |C      |
```
It came up - on the midnight clear,
```
 |F       |D7   |G    |G7
```
That glorious song of old,
```
  |C    |F    |C      |
```
From angels bending near the earth
```
 |F        |G7     |C      |
```
To touch their harps of gold.
```
      |E7   |        |Am  |
```
"Peace on the earth, good will to men,
```
    |G      |D7    |G    |G7
```
From heaven's all gracious King,"
```
 |C      |F    |C      |
```
The world in solemn stillness lay
```
 |F     |G7   |C      |
```
To hear the angels sing.

Verse 2

```
    ‖C       |F    |C      |
```
Still through the cloven skies they come
```
  |F     |D7     |G    |G7
```
With peaceful wings un - furled,
```
   |C    |F    |C    |
```
And still their heavenly music floats
```
  |F    |G7   |C      |
```
O'er all the weary world.
```
 |E7   |        |Am  |
```
A - bove its sad and lowly   plains
```
 |G     |D7    |G    |G7
```
They bend on hovering wing,
```
   |C   |F   |C    |
```
And ever o'er its Babel sounds
```
 |F     |G7   |C      |
```
The blessed angels sing.

Verse 3

```
‖C      |F      |C      |
```
Yet with the woes of sin and strife
```
 |F        |D7    |G     |G7
```
The world has suffered long,
```
  |C      |F      |C        |
```
Be - neath the heav'nly hymn have rolled
```
  |F       |G7    |C      |
```
Two thousand years of wrong,
```
  |E7    |        |Am       |
```
And warring human - kind hears not
```
 |G     |D7     |G       |G7
```
The tidings which they bring.
```
 |C      |F      |C        |
```
O hush the noise and cease your strife
```
  |F       |G7    |C      |
```
And hear the angels sing!

Verse 4

```
 ‖C      |F      |C        |
```
For lo! The days are hast'ning on,
```
 |F        |D7    |G     |G7
```
By prophets seen of old,
```
   |C      |F     |C      |
```
When with the ever - circling years
```
  |F        |G7    |C        |
```
Shall come the time fore - told,
```
   |E7     |       |Am     |
```
When peace shall over all the earth
```
 |G     |D7     |G       |G7
```
Its ancient splendors fling,
```
  |C      |F      |C        |
```
And all the world give back the song
```
    |F       |G7   |C      |      ‖
```
Which now the angels sing.

Jolly Old St. Nicholas

Traditional 19th Century American Carol

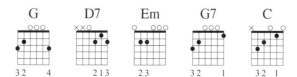

Verse 1

G |D7 |Em |G7 |
Jolly old Saint Nicholas, lean your ear this way!

C |G |D7 | |
Don't you tell a single soul what I'm going to say.

G |D7 |Em |G7 |
Christmas Eve is coming soon, now, you dear old man,

C |G |D7 |G   ‖
Whisper what you'll bring to me, tell me if you can.

Verse 2

G |D7 |Em |G7 |
When the clock is striking twelve, when I'm fast a - sleep,

C |G |D7 | |
Down the chimney broad and black, with your pack you'll creep.

G |D7 |Em |G7 |
All the stockings you will find hanging in a row.

C |G |D7 |G   ‖
Mine will be the shortest one, you'll be sure to know.

Verse 3

G |D7 |Em |G7 |
Johnny wants a pair of skates, Susy wants a sled.

C |G |D7 | |
Nellie wants a picture book, yellow, blue and red.

G |D7 |Em |G7 |
Now I think I'll leave to you what to give the rest.

C |G |D7 |G   ‖
Choose for me, dear Santa Claus, you will know the best.

O Christmas Tree

Traditional German Carol

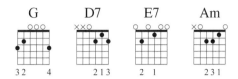

Verse 1

```
‖G          D7 |G        E7
```
O Christmas tree, O   Christmas tree,
```
  |Am        D7 |G
```
You stand in ver - dant beauty!
```
  |           D7 |G        E7
```
O Christmas tree, O   Christmas tree,
```
  |Am        D7 |G
```
You stand in ver - dant beauty!
```
  |                    |Am
```
Your boughs are green in summer's glow,
```
  |D7              |G
```
And do not fade in winter's snow.
```
D7 |G          D7 |G        E7
```
O   Christmas tree, O   Christmas tree,
```
  |Am        D7 |G
```
You stand in ver - dant beauty!

Verse 2

```
‖G          D7 |G        E7
```
O Christmas tree, O   Christmas tree,
```
  |Am        D7 |G
```
Much pleasure doth thou bring me!
```
  |           D7 |G        E7
```
O Christmas tree, O   Christmas tree,
```
  |Am        D7 |G
```
Much pleasure doth thou bring me!
```
  |          |Am
```
For every year the Christmas tree
```
  |D7             |G
```
Brings to us all both joy and glee.
```
D7 |G          D7 |G        E7
```
O   Christmas tree, O   Christmas tree,
```
  |Am        D7 |G            ‖
```
Much pleasure doth thou bring me!

Joy to the World

Words by Isaac Watts
Music by George Frideric Handel
Adapted by Lowell Mason

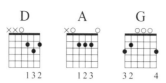

Verse 1

D | | A |D
Joy to the world! The Lord is come,
|G |A |D |
Let earth re - ceive her King.
| | | |
Let ev'ry heart pre - pare Him room,
| |
And heav'n and nature sing,
|A |
And heav'n and nature sing,
|D | | A |D ||
And heav'n and heav'n and na - ture sing.

Verse 2

D | | A |D
Joy to the world! The Sav - ior reigns,
|G |A |D |
Let men their songs em - ploy,
| | | |
While fields and floods, rocks, hills and plains
| |
Re - peat the sounding joy,
|A |
Re - peat the sounding joy,
|D | | A |D ||
Re - peat, re - peat the sound - ing joy.

Verse 3

```
D              |        |      A  |D
No more let sin and sor - row grow,
   |G       |A      |D         |
Nor thorns in - fest the ground.
   |         |        |         |
He comes to make His blessings flow
   |         |
Far as the curse is found,
   |A             |
Far as the curse is found,
   |D       |      |      A |D       ||
Far as, far as the curse is   found.
```

Verse 4

```
D            |        |      A  |D
He rules the world with truth and grace,
   |G       |A      |D         |
And makes the nations prove
   |       |      |       |       |
The glories of His righteous - ness,
   |         |
And wonders of His love,
   |A             |
And wonders of His love,
   |D       |          | A |D      ||
And wonders, wonders of His love.
```

O Come, All Ye Faithful

Music by John Francis Wade
Latin Words translated by Frederick Oakeley

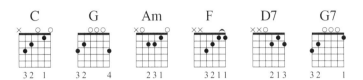

Verse 1

‖C |G |C   F |C   G
O come, all ye faithful, joyful and tri - um - phant,

 |Am D7 |G | D7 |G |
O come ye, O come ye to Beth - le - hem.

C |G   C |G   Am |G
Come and be - hold Him, born the King of angels.

Chorus 1

‖C |
O come let us a - dore Him,

| | G7
O come let us a - dore Him,

 |F |G   C   F |
O come let us a - dore Him,

C   G7 |C   ‖
Christ   the Lord.

Verse 2

C |G |C   F |C   G |
Sing, choirs of angels, sing in ex - ul - ta - tion,

Am D7 |G | D7 |G |
Sing all ye citizens of heav'n   a - bove.

C |G   C |G   Am |G
Glory to God   in   the   highest.

Chorus 2   *Repeat Chorus 1*

O Little Town of Bethlehem

Words by Phillips Brooks
Music by Lewis H. Redner

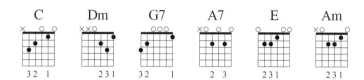

Verse 1

‖**C**　　　|**Dm**　　　|**C**　**G7**　|**C**
O little town of Bethlehem, how still we see thee lie.

|　　　**A7**　|**Dm**　　　|**C**　**G7**　|**C**
A - bove thy deep and dreamless sleep the silent stars go by.

|**Am**　　　|**E**　|**Am**　　|**E**
Yet in thy dark streets shineth the everlasting light.

|**C**　　　|**Dm**　　　|**C**　**G7**　|**C**
The hopes and fears of all the years are met in thee to - night.

Verse 2

‖**C**　　　|**Dm**　|**C**　**G7**　|**C**
For Christ is born of Mary and gather'd all a - bove.

|　　　**A7**　|**Dm**　　　|**C**　**G7**　|**C**
While mortals sleep, the angels keep their watch of wond'ring love.

|**Am**　　　|**E**　|**Am**　　|**E**
O morning stars to - gether pro - claim the holy birth!

|**C**　　　|**Dm**　　　|**C**　**G7**　|**C**　　　‖
And praises sing to God the King and peace to men on earth!

O Come, O Come, Emmanuel

Traditional Latin Text
V. 1,2 translated by John M. Neale
V. 3,4 translated by Henry S. Coffin
15th Century French Melody
Adapted by Thomas Helmore

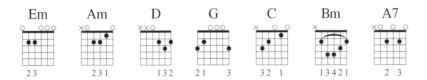

Verse 1

‖Em |Am   D |G
O come, O come, Em - man - u - el,

|Em   C |Am   Bm |Em
And ransom captive Is   -   ra - el,

|Am |Em A7 |D
That mourns in lonely ex   - ile here

|Em |Am D |G
Un - til the Son of God __ ap - pear.

Chorus 1

‖D |Em
Re - joice, re - joice!

|C   D |Em |G   C |Am Bm |Em
Em - man - u - el shall come to Thee, O Is   - ra - el!

Verse 2

‖Em |Am   D |G
O come, Thou Dayspring, come __ and cheer

|Em   C |Am   Bm |Em
Our spirits by Thine ad   - vent here;

|Am |Em A7 |D
Dis - perse the gloomy clouds __ of night,

|Em |Am D |G
And death's dark shadows put ___ to flight.

Chorus 2   *Repeat Chorus 1*

    ‖**Em** |**Am** **D** |**G**

Verse 3
O come, Thou Wisdom, from __ on high,

    |**Em** **C** |**Am Bm** |**Em**
And order all things far ____ and nigh;

    |**Am** |**Em A7** |**D**
To us the path of know - ledge show,

    |**Em** |**Am** **D** |**G**
And cause us in her ways __ to go.

Chorus 3   *Repeat Chorus 1*

    ‖**Em** |**Am** **D** |**G**

Verse 4
O come, desire of na - tions, bind

    |**Em** **C** |**Am Bm** |**Em**
All people in one heart __ and mind;

    |**Am** |**Em A7** |**D**
Bid envy, strife, and quar - rels cease;

    |**Em** |**Am** **D** |**G**
Fill the whole world with heav - en's peace.

Chorus 4   *Repeat Chorus 1*

    ‖**Em** |**Am D** |**G**

Verse 5
O come, Thou Key of Da - vid, come,

    |**Em C** |**Am Bm** |**Em**
And open wide our heav - 'nly home.

    |**Am** |**Em A7** |**D**
Make safe the way that leads __ on high,

    |**Em** |**Am D** |**G**
And close the path to mis - er - y.

Chorus 5   *Repeat Chorus 1*

O Holy Night

French Words by Placide Cappeau
English Words by John S. Dwight
Music by Adolphe Adam

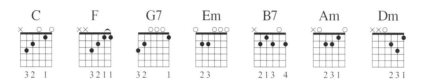

C   F   G7   Em   B7   Am   Dm

Verse 1

C | |**F** |**C** |
O holy night, the stars are brightly shin - ing,

| |**G7** |**C** | |
It is the night of the dear Saviour's birth.

| |**F** |**C** |
Long lay the world in sin and error pin - ing

|**Em** |**B7** |**Em** |
Till He ap - peared and the soul felt its worth.

|**G7** | |**C** |
A thrill of hope the weary world re - joices,

|**G7** | |**C** | |
For yonder breaks a new and glorious morn.

Am | |**Em** |
Fall   on your knees!

|**Dm** | |**Am** |
O hear   the angel voic - es!

|**C** |**G7** |**C** |**F**
O night   di - vine!

|**C** |**G7** |**C** |
O night   when Christ was born,

|**G7** | |**C** |**F**
O night   di - vine!

|**C** |**G7** |**C** | ‖
O night,   O night di - vine!

Verse 2

```
C              |        |F        |C      |
Truly He taught us to love one an - oth - er.
         |              |G7       |C      |         |
His law is love and His gospel is peace.
              |              |F        |C        |
Chains shall He break, for the slave is our broth - er,
         |Em        |B7       |Em        |
And in His name all op - pression shall cease.
    |G7      |     |C          |
Sweet hymns of joy in grateful chorus raise we.
    |G7      |     |C          |         |
Let all with - in us praise His holy name.
Am    |      |Em   |
Christ is the Lord,
    |Dm   |              |Am  |
Oh, praise His name for - ev - er!
    |C   |G7   |C   |F      |
His pow'r    and glo - ry
C  |G7              |C        |
Ev  -  ermore pro - claim!
    |G7   |     |C   |F      |
His pow'r and glo   -   ry
C  |G7              |C   |     ‖
Ev - ermore pro - claim!
```

Parade of the Wooden Soldiers

English Lyrics by Ballard MacDonald
Music by Leon Jessel

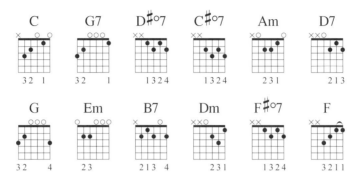

Verse 1

‖**C** |**G7**
The toy shop door is locked up tight

|**C**   **D#°7** |**G7**
And every - thing is quiet for the night,

|**C**   **C#°7** |**G7**
When sudden - ly the clock strikes twelve;

|**Am D7** |**G**
The fun's be - gun.

Verse 2

‖**C** |**G7**
The dolls are in their best arrayed;

|**C**   **D#°7** |**G7**
There's going to be a wonderful parade.

|**C**   **C#°7** |**G7**
Hark to the drum, "Oh! Here they come,"

|**Am D7** |**G**   ‖
Cries ev - 'ry - one.

Chorus 1

C | |
Here them all cheering, now they are nearing;

|G7 |
There's the captain stiff as starch.

| |
Bayonets flashing, music is crashing

|C |
As the wooden soldiers march.

| |
Sabres a-clinking, soldiers a-winking

|Em |
At each pretty little maid.

|
Here they come! Here they come!

|
Here they come! Here they come!

B7 |Em   G7 ‖
Wooden soldiers on pa - rade.

Chorus 2

C | |
Daylignt is creeping, dollies are sleeping

|G7 |
In the toy shop window fast:

| |
Soldiers are jolly, think of each dolly

|C |
Dreaming of the night that's past.

| |
When in the morning, without warning,

|Dm |
Toyman pulls the window shade.

F#°7 |C |F   G7 |C   ‖
There's no sign the Wood Brigade was ever out up - on pa - rade.

Silent Night

Words by Joseph Mohr
Translated by John F. Young
Music by Franz X. Gruber

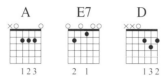

Verse 1

A | |
Silent night, holy night!

E7 |**A** |
All is calm, all is bright.

D |**A** |
Round yon virgin Mother and Child.

D |**A** |
Holy Infant, so tender and mild,

E7 |**A** |
Sleep in heavenly peace.

    E7 |**A** ||
Sleep in heavenly peace.

Verse 2

A | |
Silent night, holy night!

E7 |A |
Shepherds quake at the sight.

D |A |
Glories stream from heaven afar.

D |A |
Heav'nly hosts sing Alleluia,

E7 |A |
Christ, the Savior, is born.

E7 |A ‖
Christ, the Savior, is born.

Verse 3

A | |
Silent night, holy night!

E7 |A |
Son of God, love's pure light.

D |A |
Radiant beams from Thy holy face,

D |A |
With the dawn of re - deeming grace,

E7 |A |
Jesus, Lord at Thy birth.

E7 |A ‖
Jesus, Lord at Thy birth.

Star of the East

Words by George Cooper
Music by Amanda Kennedy

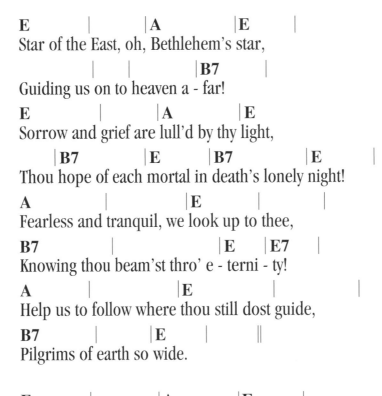

Verse 1

E | |A |E |
Star of the East, oh, Bethlehem's star,

| | |B7 |
Guiding us on to heaven a - far!

E | |A |E
Sorrow and grief are lull'd by thy light,

|B7 |E |B7 |E |
Thou hope of each mortal in death's lonely night!

A | |E | |
Fearless and tranquil, we look up to thee,

B7 | |E |E7 |
Knowing thou beam'st thro' e - terni - ty!

A | |E | |
Help us to follow where thou still dost guide,

B7 | |E | ||
Pilgrims of earth so wide.

Verse 2

E | |A |E |
Star of the East, thou hope of the soul,

| | |B7 |
While round us here the dark billows roll.

E | |A |E
Lead us from sin to glory a - far,

|B7 |E |B7 |E
Thou star of the East, thou sweet Bethl'em's star.

| |B7 |E A |E
Oh star that leads to God a - bove,

|B7 |E |B7 |
Whose rays are peace and joy and love.

|E |B7 |E A |E
Watch o'er us still 'til life hath ceased.

|B7 |E |B7 |E ||
Beam on, bright star, sweet Bethlehem star!

Toyland
from BABES IN TOYLAND

Words by Glen MacDonough
Music by Victor Herbert

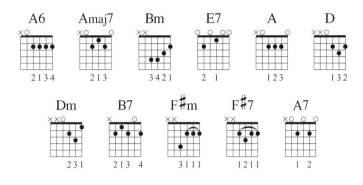

Verse 1

A6　　　|**Amaj7**　|
Toyland! Toyland!

Bm E7　　　|**A**　　　|
Little girl and boyland.

D　　　**Dm**　　　|**A**　
While you dwell with - in it,

　　　　　|**B7**　　　|**E7**　　　　||
You are ever happy then.

Verse 2

A6　　　　|**Amaj7**　|
Childhood's Joyland,

Bm　　**E7**　|**A**　　　|
Mystical, merry Toyland!
F♯m　　　　　|
Once you pass its borders
F♯7　|**Bm**　　**E7**　|**A**
You can never re - turn a - gain.

Bridge

　　　　||**D**　　　　　|**A7**
When you've grown up, my dears,

　　　|**D**　　　|**A7**
And are as old as I,

　　　|**D**　　　|**Bm**
You'll often ponder on the years

　　　|**E7**　　　|**A7**
That roll so swiftly by, my dears,

　　　|**D**　　**A7**　|**D**　　**E7**　　||
That roll so swifty by.

Verse 3

Repeat Verse 2

Sussex Carol

Traditional English Carol

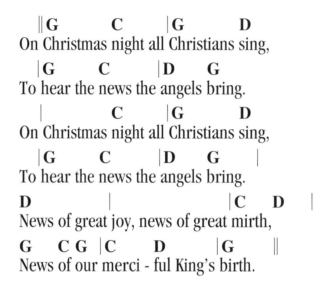

Verse 1

```
‖G        C      |G          D
```
On Christmas night all Christians sing,
```
 |G     C        |D     G
```
To hear the news the angels bring.
```
 |           C      |G          D
```
On Christmas night all Christians sing,
```
 |G     C        |D     G      |
```
To hear the news the angels bring.
```
D            |               |C    D   |
```
News of great joy, news of great mirth,
```
G    C G |C      D        |G        ‖
```
News of our merci - ful King's birth.

Interlude 1

```
|G      C   |G      D   |G
```

Verse 2

```
    ‖G        C      |G          D
```
Then why should men on earth be so sad
```
     |G     C     |D     G
```
Since our Re - deemer made us glad?
```
    |           C      |G          D
```
Then why should men on earth be so sad
```
     |G     C     |D     G
```
Since our Re - deemer made us glad;
```
D            |               |C    D   |
```
When from our sin He set us free,
```
G  C G |C      D      |G        ‖
```
All for to gain our liber - ty?

Interlude 2   *Repeat Interlude 1*

Verse 3

```
  ‖G      C      |G        D
When sin de - parts be - fore His grace,
   |G         C         |D    G
Then our life and health come in its place.
   |        C      |G        D
When sin de - parts be - fore His grace,
   |G         C          |D    G    |
Then our life and health come in its place.
D        |                |C    D    |
Angels and men with joy may sing,
G  C  G |C      D          |G        ‖
All for to  see the new - born King.
```

Interlude 3   *Repeat Interlude 1*

Verse 4

```
  ‖G    C        |G        D
All out of darkness we have light,
   |G       C    |D      G
Which made the angels sing this night.
   |      C      |G      D
All out of darkness we have light,
   |G       C    |D      G
Which made the angels sing this night.
  D      |                |C    D    |
"Glory to God and peace to men,
G   C   G |C    D        |G        ‖
Now and for - ever - more. A - men."
```

Outro |G   C |G   D |G   ‖

The Twelve Days of Christmas

Traditional English Carol

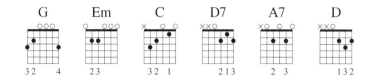

Verse 1

```
        ‖G        Em       |C        D7   G
On the first day of Christmas, my true love gave to me:
   |     C    G   D7 |G
A par - tridge in a pear tree.
```

Verse 2

```
        ‖G          Em        |C        D7    G     |
On the second day of Christmas, my true love gave to me:
D7
Two turtle doves,
     |G   C    G   D7 |G
And a par - tridge in a pear tree.
```

Verse 3

```
        ‖G         Em        |C       D7    G     |
On the third day of Christmas, my true love gave to me:
D7                 |
Three French hens, two turtle doves,
     |G   C    G   D7 |G
And a par - tridge in a pear tree.
```

Verse 4

```
        ‖G          Em        |C        D7    G     |
On the fourth day of Christmas, my true love gave to me:
D7             |              |
Four calling birds, three French hens, two turtle doves,
     |G   C    G   D7 |G
And a par - tridge in a pear tree.
```

Verse 5

```
        ‖G        Em       |C       D7    G     |
On the fifth day of Christmas, my true love gave to me:
     A7    |D       |
Five golden rings.
G              |C             |A7      D7
Four calling birds, three French hens, two turtle doves,
     |G   C    G   D7 |G
And a par - tridge in a pear tree.
```

Verse 6

```
        ‖G          Em        |C        D7      G         |
On the sixth day of Christmas, my true love gave to me:
D7                        |
Six geese a laying,
G   A7    |D        |
Five golden rings.
G               |C                 |A7        D7
Four calling birds, three French hens, two turtle doves,
     |G    C    G  D7 |G
And a par - tridge in a pear tree.
```

Verse 7

```
        ‖G          Em        |C        D7      G         |
On the seventh day of Christmas, my true love gave to me:
D7                       |                    |
Seven Swans a swimming, six geese a laying,
G   A7    |D        |
Five golden rings.
G               |C                 |A7        D7
Four calling birds, three French hens, two turtle doves,
     |G    C    G  D7 |G
And a par - tridge in a pear tree.
```

Verse 8

```
        ‖G          Em        |C        D7      G         |
On the eighth day of Christmas, my true love gave to me:
D7                  |                    |              |
Eight maids a milking, seven swans a swimming, six geese a laying,
G   A7    |D        |
Five golden rings.
G               |C                 |A7        D7
Four calling birds, three French hens, two turtle doves,
     |G    C    G  D7 |G
And a par - tridge in a pear tree.
```

Verse 9

```
        ‖G          Em        |C        D7      G         |
On the ninth day of Christmas, my true love gave to me:
D7                  |
Nine ladies dancing,

                       |                    |              |
Eight maids a milking, seven swans a swimming, six geese a laying,
G   A7    |D        |
Five golden rings.
G               |C                 |A7        D7
Four calling birds, three French hens, two turtle doves,
     |G    C    G  D7 |G
And a par - tridge in a pear tree.
```

Verse 10

```
           ‖G          Em        |C       D7      G        |
On the tenth day of Christmas, my true love gave to me:
D7                         |                       |
Ten lords a leaping, nine ladies dancing,

                  |                        |                 |
Eight maids a milking, seven swans a swimming, six geese a laying,
G   A7   |D       |
Five golden rings.
G                 |C                 |A7        D7
Four calling birds, three French hens, two turtle doves,
      |G    C    G  D7 |G
And a par - tridge in a pear tree.
```

Verse 11

```
           ‖G          Em        |C       D7      G        |
On the 'leventh day of Christmas, my true love gave to me:
 D7                  |                   |                 |
'Leven pipers piping, ten lords a leaping, nine ladies dancing,

                  |                        |                 |
Eight maids a milking, seven swans a swimming, six geese a laying,
G   A7   |D       |
Five golden rings.
G                 |C                 |A7        D7
Four calling birds, three French hens, two turtle doves,
      |G    C    G  D7 |G
And a par - tridge in a pear tree.
```

Verse 12

```
           ‖G          Em        |C       D7      G        |
On the twelfth day of Christmas, my true love gave to me:
 D7                         |
Twelve drummers drumming,

                  |                   |                 |
'Leven pipers piping, ten lords a leaping, nine ladies dancing,

                  |                        |                 |
Eight maids a milking, seven swans a swimming, six geese a laying,
G   A7   |D       |
Five golden rings.
G                 |C                 |A7        D7
Four calling birds, three French hens, two turtle doves,
      |G    C    G  D7 |G              ‖
And a par - tridge in a pear tree.
```

We Wish You a Merry Christmas

Traditional English Folksong

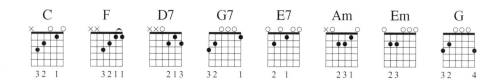

Verse 1

         ‖**C** |**F**
We wish you a merry Christmas,
     |**D7** |**G7**
We wish you a merry Christmas,
     |**E7** |**Am**
We wish you a merry Christmas,
    |**F**   **G7** |**C**
And a happy New Year.

Bridge 1

        ‖**Am** |**Em**
Good tidings to you,
     |**D7** |**G**
Wher - ever you are,
    |**C** |
Good tidings for Christmas
    |**F**   **G7** |**C**
And a happy New Year!

Verse 2

         ‖**C** |**F**
We all know that Santa's coming,
     |**D7** |**G7**
We all know that Santa's coming,
     |**E7** |**Am**
We all know that Santa's coming,
    |**F**   **G7** |**C**
And soon will be here.

Bridge 2   *Repeat Bridge 1*

Verse 3   *Repeat Verse 1*

Up on the Housetop

Words and Music by
B.R. Hanby

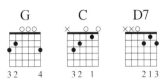

Verse 1

G | |
Up on the housetop reindeer pause,
C **G** |**D7** |
Out jumps good old Santa Claus.
G | |
Down through the chimney with lots of toys,
C **G** |**D7** **G** ‖
All for the little ones, Christmas joys.

Chorus 1

C |**G** |
Ho, ho, ho, who wouldn't go?
D7 |**G** |
Ho, ho, ho, who wouldn't go?
|**C** |
Up on the housetop, click, click, click.
G |**D7** **G** ‖
Down through the chimney with good Saint Nick.

Verse 2

G | |
First comes the stocking of little Nell,
C   G |D7 |
Oh, dear Santa, fill it well.
G | |
Give her a dollie that laughs and cries,
C   G |D7   G   ‖
One that will open and shut her eyes.

Chorus 2   *Repeat Chorus 1*

Verse 3

G | |
Next comes the stocking of little Will,
C   G |D7 |
Oh, just see what a glorious fill!
G | |
Here is a hammer and lots of tacks,
C   G |D7   G   ‖
Also a ball and a whip that cracks.

Chorus 3   *Repeat Chorus 1*

We Three Kings of Orient Are

Words and Music by
John H. Hopkins, Jr.

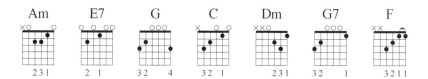

Verse 1

Am | |**E7** |**Am** |
We three kings of orient are

| |**E7** |**Am** |
Bearing gifts we traverse a - far,

|**G** |**C** | |
Field and fountain, moor and mountain,

Dm |**E7** |**Am** |
Following yonder star.

Chorus 1

G7 ‖**C** | |**F** |**C** |
O,   star of wonder, star of night,

| |**F** |**C** |
Star with royal beauty bright,

Am |**G** |**F** |**G** |
Westward leading, still pro - ceeding,

C | |**F** |**C** ‖
Guide us to thy perfect light.

Verse 2

Am | |**E7** |**Am** |
Born a King on Bethlehem plain,

| |**E7** |**Am** |
Gold I bring to crown Him a - gain.

|**G** |**C** | |
King for - ever, ceasing never,

Dm |**E7** |**Am** |
Over us all to reign.

Chorus 2   *Repeat Chorus 1*

Verse 3
```
Am      |         |E7       |Am     |
```
Frankin - cense to offer have I,
```
        |         |E7  |Am     |
```
Incense owns a Deity nigh.
```
              |G        |C       |       |
```
Prayer and praising, all men raising,
```
Dm            |E7        |Am      |
```
Worship Him, God most high.

Chorus 3   *Repeat Chorus 1*

Verse 4
```
Am      |         |E7       |Am     |
```
Myrrh is mine. It's bitter per - fume
```
        |         |E7       |Am      |
```
Breathes a life of gathering gloom.
```
              |G        |C       |       |
```
Sorrowing, sighing, bleeding, dying,
```
Dm            |E7        |Am      |
```
Sealed in the stone-cold tomb.

Chorus 4   *Repeat Chorus 1*

Verse 5
```
Am      |         |E7       |Am      |
```
Glorious now, be - hold Him a - rise,
```
        |         |E7  |Am      |
```
King and God and Sacri - fice!
```
      |G  |C  |        |
```
Alle - luia, alle - luia,
```
Dm      |E7      |Am      |
```
Earth to heaven re - plies.

Chorus 5   *Repeat Chorus 1*

What Child Is This?

Words by William C. Dix
16th Century English Melody

Verse 1

‖**Am** | |**G** |
What child is this, who, laid to rest,

|**F** | |**E7** |
On Mary's lap is sleep - ing,

|**Am** | |**G** |
Whom angels greet with anthems sweet

|**F** |**E7** |**Am** | ‖
While shepherds watch are keep - ing?

Chorus 1

C | |**G** |**Em**
This, this is Christ the King

|**Am** |**F** |**E7** | |
Whom shepherds guard and angels sing:

C | |**G** |**Em**
Haste, haste to bring Him laud,

|**Am** |**E7** |**Am** |
The Babe, the Son of Mar - y.

Verse 2

```
   ‖Am   |        |G·        |
Why lies He in such mean es - tate
     |F    |        |E7  |
Where ox and ass are feed - ing?
     |Am   |        |G    |
Good Christian, fear, for sinners here
     |F    |E7   |Am   |      ‖
The silent Word is plead - ing.
```

Chorus 2   *Repeat Chorus 1*

Verse 3

```
   ‖Am   |        |G        |
So bring Him incense, gold and myrrh,
     |F    |        |E7  |
Come, peasant king, to own  Him.
     |Am   |        |G    |
The King of kings sal - vation brings,
     |F    |E7   |Am   |      ‖
Let loving hearts en - throne Him.
```

Chorus 3   *Repeat Chorus 1*

STRUM & SING

Lyrics, chord symbols, and guitar chord diagrams for your favorite songs.

GUITAR

ACOUSTIC CLASSICS
00191891 .... $14.99

ADELE
00159855 .... $12.99

SARA BAREILLES
00102354 .... $12.99

THE BEATLES
00172234 .... $16.99

BLUES
00159335 .... $12.99

ZAC BROWN BAND
02501620 .... $14.99

COLBIE CAILLAT
02501725 .... $14.99

CAMPFIRE FOLK SONGS
02500686 .... $14.99

CHART HITS OF 2014-2015
00142554 .... $12.99

CHART HITS OF 2015-2016
00156248 .... $12.99

BEST OF KENNY CHESNEY
00142457 .... $14.99

CHRISTMAS SONGS
00171332 .... $14.99

KELLY CLARKSON
00146384 .... $14.99

COFFEEHOUSE SONGS FOR GUITAR
00285991 .... $14.99

LEONARD COHEN
00265489 .... $14.99

JOHN DENVER COLLECTION
02500632 .... $12.99

DISNEY
00233900 .... $16.99

EAGLES
00157994 .... $12.99

EASY ACOUSTIC SONGS
00125478 .... $14.99

THE 5 CHORD SONGBOOK
02501718 .... $12.99

FOLK SONGS
02501482 .... $10.99

FOLK/ROCK FAVORITES
02501669 .... $12.99

FOUR CHORD SONGS
00249581 .... $14.99

THE 4 CHORD SONGBOOK
02501533 .... $12.99

THE 4-CHORD COUNTRY SONGBOOK
00114936 .... $15.99

THE GREATEST SHOWMAN
00278383 .... $14.99

HAMILTON
00217116 .... $14.99

JACK JOHNSON
02500858 .... $17.99

ROBERT JOHNSON
00191890 .... $12.99

CAROLE KING
00115243 .... $10.99

BEST OF GORDON LIGHTFOOT
00139393 .... $14.99

DAVE MATTHEWS BAND
02501078 .... $10.95

JOHN MAYER
02501636 .... $10.99

INGRID MICHAELSON
02501634 .... $10.99

THE MOST REQUESTED SONGS
02501748 .... $12.99

JASON MRAZ
02501452 .... $14.99

PRAISE & WORSHIP
00152381 .... $12.99

ELVIS PRESLEY
00198890 .... $12.99

QUEEN
00218578 .... $12.99

ROCK AROUND THE CLOCK
00103625 .... $12.99

ROCK BALLADS
02500872 .... $9.95

ROCKETMAN
00300469 .... $17.99

ED SHEERAN
00152016 .... $14.99

THE 6 CHORD SONGBOOK
02502277 .... $12.99

CAT STEVENS
00116827 .... $14.99

TAYLOR SWIFT
00159856 .... $12.99

THE 3 CHORD SONGBOOK
00211634 .... $10.99

TODAY'S HITS
00119301 .... $12.99

TOP CHRISTIAN HITS
00156331 .... $12.99

TOP HITS OF 2016
00194288 .... $12.99

KEITH URBAN
00118558 .... $14.99

THE WHO
00103667 .... $12.99

YESTERDAY
00301629 .... $14.99

NEIL YOUNG – GREATEST HITS
00138270 .... $14.99

UKULELE

THE BEATLES
00233899 .... $16.99

COLBIE CAILLAT
02501731 .... $10.99

COFFEEHOUSE SONGS FOR UKULELE
00138238 .... $14.99

JOHN DENVER
02501694 .... $10.99

FOLK ROCK FAVORITES FOR UKULELE
00114600 .... $12.99

THE 4-CHORD UKULELE SONGBOOK
00114331 .... $14.99

JACK JOHNSON
02501702 .... $19.99

JOHN MAYER
02501706 .... $10.99

INGRID MICHAELSON
02501741 .... $12.99

THE MOST REQUESTED SONGS
02501453 .... $14.99

JASON MRAZ
02501753 .... $14.99

SING-ALONG SONGS
02501710 .... $15.99

HAL•LEONARD®

www.halleonard.com
Visit our website to see full song lists.

AUTHENTIC CHORDS • ORIGINAL KEYS • COMPLETE SONGS

The *Strum It* series lets players strum the chords and sing along with their favorite hits. Each song has been selected because it can be played with regular open chords, barre chords, or other moveable chord types. Guitarists can simply play the rhythm, or play and sing along through the entire song. All songs are shown in their original keys complete with chords, strum patterns, melody and lyrics. Wherever possible, the chord voicings from the recorded versions are notated.

THE BEACH BOYS' GREATEST HITS
00699357............................ $12.95

THE BEATLES FAVORITES
00699249............................$15.99

VERY BEST OF JOHNNY CASH
00699514............................$14.99

CELTIC GUITAR SONGBOOK
00699265............................$12.99

CHRISTMAS SONGS FOR GUITAR
00699247............................$10.95

CHRISTMAS SONGS WITH 3 CHORDS
00699487............................$9.99

VERY BEST OF ERIC CLAPTON
00699560............................$12.95

JIM CROCE – CLASSIC HITS
00699269............................$10.95

DISNEY FAVORITES
00699171............................$14.99

MELISSA ETHERIDGE GREATEST HITS
00699518............................$12.99

FAVORITE SONGS WITH 3 CHORDS
00699112............................$10.99

FAVORITE SONGS WITH 4 CHORDS
00699270............................$8.95

FIRESIDE SING-ALONG
00699273............................$12.99

FOLK FAVORITES
00699517............................$8.95

THE GUITAR STRUMMERS' ROCK SONGBOOK
00701678............................$14.99

BEST OF WOODY GUTHRIE
00699496............................$12.95

JOHN HIATT COLLECTION
00699398............................$17.99

THE VERY BEST OF BOB MARLEY
00699524............................$14.99

A MERRY CHRISTMAS SONGBOOK
00699211............................$10.99

MORE FAVORITE SONGS WITH 3 CHORDS
00699532............................$9.99

THE VERY BEST OF TOM PETTY
00699336............................$15.99

BEST OF GEORGE STRAIT
00699235............................$16.99

TAYLOR SWIFT FOR ACOUSTIC GUITAR
00109717............................$16.99

BEST OF HANK WILLIAMS JR.
00699224............................$16.99

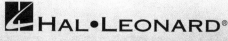

Prices, contents & availability subject to change without notice.

Visit Hal Leonard online at
www.halleonard.com

Guitar Chord Songbooks

Each 6" x 9" book includes complete lyrics, chord symbols, and guitar chord diagrams.

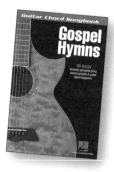
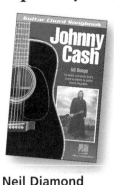
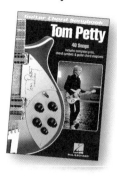

Acoustic Hits
00701787 .... $14.99

Acoustic Rock
00699540 .... $19.99

Alabama
00699914 .... $14.95

The Beach Boys
00699566 .... $17.99

The Beatles (A-I)
00699558 .... $17.99

The Beatles (J-Y)
00699562 .... $17.99

Bluegrass
00702585 .... $14.99

Johnny Cash
00699648 .... $17.99

Children's Songs
00699539 .... $16.99

Christmas Carols
00699536 .... $12.99

Christmas Songs – 2nd Edition
00119911 .... $14.99

Eric Clapton
00699567 .... $16.99

Classic Rock
00699598 .... $16.99

Coffeehouse Hits
00703318 .... $14.99

Country
00699534 .... $14.99

Country Favorites
00700609 .... $14.99

Country Hits
00140859 .... $14.99

Country Standards
00700608 .... $12.95

Cowboy Songs
00699636 .... $15.99

Creedence Clearwater Revival
00701786 .... $15.99

Jim Croce
00148087 .... $14.99

Crosby, Stills & Nash
00701609 .... $12.99

John Denver
02501697 .... $16.99

Neil Diamond
00700606 .... $17.99

Disney – 2nd Edition
00295786 .... $17.99

The Best of Bob Dylan
14037617 .... $17.99

Eagles
00122917 .... $16.99

Early Rock
00699916 .... $14.99

Folksongs
00699541 .... $14.99

Folk Pop Rock
00699651 .... $15.99

40 Easy Strumming Songs
00115972 .... $15.99

Four Chord Songs
00701611 .... $14.99

Glee
00702501 .... $14.99

Gospel Hymns
00700463 .... $14.99

Grand Ole Opry®
00699885 .... $16.95

Grateful Dead
00139461 .... $14.99

Green Day
00103074 .... $14.99

Guitar Chord Songbook White Pages
00702609 .... $29.99

Irish Songs
00701044 .... $14.99

Michael Jackson
00137847 .... $14.99

Billy Joel
00699632 .... $16.99

Elton John
00699732 .... $15.99

Ray LaMontagne
00130337 .... $12.99

Latin Songs
00700973 .... $14.99

Love Songs
00701043 .... $14.99

Bob Marley
00701704 .... $14.99

Bruno Mars
00125332 .... $12.99

Paul McCartney
00385035 .... $16.95

Steve Miller
00701146 .... $12.99

Modern Worship
00701801 .... $16.99

Motown
00699734 .... $17.99

Willie Nelson
00148273 .... $15.99

Nirvana
00699762 .... $16.99

Roy Orbison
00699752 .... $16.99

Peter, Paul & Mary
00103013 .... $14.99

Tom Petty
00699883 .... $15.99

Pink Floyd
00139116 .... $14.99

Pop/Rock
00699538 .... $16.99

Praise & Worship
00699634 .... $14.99

Elvis Presley
00699633 .... $15.99

Queen
00702395 .... $14.99

Red Hot Chili Peppers
00699710 .... $17.99

The Rolling Stones
00137716 .... $17.99

Bob Seger
00701147 .... $12.99

Carly Simon
00121011 .... $14.99

Sting
00699921 .... $14.99

Taylor Swift
00263755 .... $16.99

Three Chord Acoustic Songs
00123860 .... $14.99

Three Chord Songs
00699720 .... $14.99

Two-Chord Songs
00119236 .... $14.99

U2
00137744 .... $14.99

Hank Williams
00700607 .... $16.99

Stevie Wonder
00120862 .... $14.99

Neil Young–Decade
00700464 .... $15.99

Prices, contents, and availability subject to change without notice.

Visit Hal Leonard online at **www.halleonard.com**